Stanzas in America

STANZAS IN AMERICA

by

Gilbert Allen

Measure Press
Savannah, Georgia

Printed in the United States of America
First Edition

The text of this book is composed in Baskerville.
Composition by R.G.
Manufacturing by Ingram.

Allen, Gilbert
Stanzas in America / by Gilbert Allen — 1st ed.

ISBN-13: 978-1-939574-42-8
ISBN-10: 1-939574-42-0
Library of Congress Control Number: 2025945963

Measure Press
2 Longberry Lane
Savannah, GA 31419
http://www.measurepress.com/measure/

Acknowledgments

The author wishes to thank the editors of the publications in which the following poems first appeared, sometimes in slightly different form:

Appalachian Journal: "UNLIMITED OPPORTUNITIES STATEWIDE"; "Marcescence in March"; "Clearcut"
Beyond Forgetting: "How"
Cumberland Poetry Review: "'It . . . Matters to History but Not to Poetry'"
Eclectica: "Elegy"
Emrys Journal: "Manikins for Dummies"
EPOCH: "For the Lost Fathers"
Fall Lines: "Fruit"
First Things: "Optics"
floor_plan: "Stanzas in America"
Found Anew: "Swamp Rabbit Parking Lot, Train in Background"
FutureCycle: "Finished"
Jiggery-Pokery Semicentennial: "Yes"
Kakalak: "The Janitors' Concert"; "The Mass of August"
Light: "Burgerdämmerung"
Measure: "Dover Beach (Barbados)"; "Gas Ghazaller"; "Tech Support"
New Verse News: "Silencer Night (or, An American Xmas)"; "Roadside Calvary, Flagpole Presiding"; "Lessons from the Dead"; "Mending News"
Orchards Poetry Journal: "Take One"; "Customer Assistance"; "Organ Recitals"

Pedestal Magazine: "Cross Dressers"; "OUTLOOK FOR TEMPORAL CREATURES BLEAK"
Pembroke Magazine: "History"
Poem: "Hempstead, 1959"; "Shooting the Snowman"
Poeming Pigeon: "Once More, *The Sound of Music*"
Road Not Taken: "A Visitation"
Salt: "A Short History of Stone Age Rock"
Sewanee Theological Review: "Serving Free Lunches in the Basement of the Travelers Rest United Methodist Church"; "Family Dining"
Shenandoah: "Ornament"; "Fearful Symmetry"
Smartish Pace: "Black Friday at Inner Spring"
South Carolina Review: "The Very Last Supper"; "Touring the Holocaust Museum with Martha Stewart"; "The Great American Sonnet"; "Belief"
Southern Review: "For Our 70th Birthdays"; "Here"
Southern Voices: Fifty Contemporary Poets: "Invitation"; "The Heaven of Mistaken Assumptions"
Strong Verse: "Second Thoughts"
Theology, Vocation, Social Justice: "Green Hair"
Tipton Poetry Journal: "SPEED LIMIT ENFORCED BY AIRCRAFT"; "Manic Regressive"
Town Creek Poetry: "Vigor"
Zone 3: "Joyville"

"The Very Last Supper," "'It . . . Matters to History but Not to Poetry,'" "Optics," and "Touring the Holocaust Museum with Martha Stewart" appeared in *Body Parts*, a chapbook published by Stepping Stones Press.

"Clearcut" and "For the Lost Fathers" were reprinted in *Southern Voices*.

"'It . . . Matters to History but Not to Poetry'" was featured on *Your Daily Poem.*

"Manikins for Dummies" received the Nancy Dew Taylor Poetry Award from the *Emrys Journal.*

The cover photo, "Swamp Rabbit Parking Lot, Train in Background," is from the South Caroliniana Library Digital Collections, University of South Carolina, Columbia, SC.

For Joni and David

CONTENTS

I. *The Heaven of Mistaken Assumptions*

II. *How*

III. *Green Hair*

IV. *Fearful Symmetry*

V. *Joyville*

I

The Heaven of Mistaken Assumptions

Take One

Zebras, xylophones at rest,
graze green scores — bored, unimpressed.
Lions laze like useless lyres,
terminally uninspired.

Hippos float like grand pianos
covered with whole notes of guano.
Oxpeckers play hidebound keys
chopsticking their ticks and fleas.

Cheetah's cello, scales ascending
bows his way toward an ending.
Antelope's lame, hopeless solo
flops — her futile to-and-fro, slows.

Hyenas harmonize their grins.
Vultures soar like violins.

History

1.
As Sachsenhausen's "volunteers,"
Jehovah's Witnesses
could leave — as soon as they *Sieg Heil*'d
in front of the SS.

They didn't. Heinrich Himmler praised
their honor, to beget
Schutzstaffel loyalty. Behold!
Unguarded, they stay put!

Unshakable faith! Discipline!
Their heavenly worldview
succeeded marvelously in
prolonging World War Two.

What's wrong with doubletalk?
Why didn't they just walk?

2.
Transmuting everyone and every
thing, like television,
evil savors virtue for
the end — the olive in

the martini, olive saplings
turned into the iron
that defended Reichstag ruins
to the last child-man.

Jehovah? Loyal witnessing?
They tell inheritors
just this: Good isn't always Good.
Behold its double doors:

One's what you do, unwatched.
The other? Not so much.

"It. . .Matters to History but Not to Poetry"

— M. H. Abrams (General Editor, The Norton Anthology of English Literature*), on Keats's erroneous assertion that Cortez discovered the Pacific*

Although I've switched kin and ken
on occasion, taken Mondays
for Tuesdays, moved convenience stores
from one intersection to

the next, changed dolls
to inflatable dummies, even
misremembered grand
-father for -mother, I'd still like to think

certain matters deserve respect.
Making love or money,
taking a shower or a shellacking,
feeling the rapture

or the rupture,
all make a difference.
Gentle Balboa broke ass, not donkey,
humping to Darien — only to have his head

handed to him, like poetic justice.
What a pity his name should be writ
in water — as stout Coleridge
so memorably never put it.

Stanzas in America

With DIRECTV, you can watch, pause,
and continue in any room!

The hooker's bleeding, but she's still alive —
eyes widening to a saw's electric shriek,
bikini duct-taped to an operating
table. Pause. Let's stroll into the kitchen

for what the linguist Hayakawa called
"a first-rate piece of dead cow" — filet mignon,
rare, on a fresh baguette — and chew our way
into the bedroom, licking our fingers clean.

Click to continue. Gloved hands lift the gag
from her smeared lips, then slow down metal teeth
so we can hear her scream. Till he reminds her
Soundproof room. This time, we stop the teeth,

yawning into the power bath, to floss
before we try that new peroxide rinse
and resurrect the scene above our tub.
The psychopath's still waiting, just for us.

Swamp Rabbit Parking Lot, Train in Background

The cop car tells me we're in Echo Valley,
1964 or thereabouts:
TERRITORIAL MARSHAL mimicking
the Golden Age of Television cowboys

and theme parks like the one outside the frame.
The hitching rails, the sanitized saloons,
mock gunfights, hangings interrupted by
a shot that shears the rope. But inside? There's

a man half cut off by the western edge
and a short woman, half cut off by him.
She holds a wicker handbag big enough
to get her started in another life.

The train's first car looks full; the second, empty.
Beyond the treeline, storm clouds fill the sky.
But in the foreground's world of gasoline
there's still enough sunlight to cast deep shadows.

Someone, perhaps the marshal, rests his palm
upon his trusty hood, as if remembering
a horse. And at the eastern edge, behind
the Rambler wagon, a toddler in short pants

stands with his own incongruous dignity.
To onlookers, the mom holding his hand
could be Camelot's Jackie on a bad
hair day. She gazes toward the ancient train

filling the past and future with its smoke.

Silencer Night
(or, An American Xmas)

> *On August 1st, Defense Distributed plans to release downloadable gun blueprints to make untraceable, undetectable, plastic 3D printed guns.*
>
> — Change.org

Timothy was sound asleep
beside his snoring pup
when at 11:55
his cellphone woke him up.

The toddler got out of bed
exactly as he'd planned
and tiptoed quickly down the stairs
to claim his contraband.

Suspended from the fireplace
(thoughtfully unlit)
a pair of portly pantaloons
seemed just about to split.

And nearly touching the gas logs
a pair of blackened boots
hung with heavy dignity
in artificial soot.

He waited on the bottom step
for Santa to emerge.
Although the toddler longed to speak,
Timothy fought the urge.

Saint Nicholas beheld the tree
besieged by piles of stuff.
He rubbed his beard. He checked his list.
"I think Tim has enough."

He opened his Emergency Sack
to cram some presents *in*.
A little face froze into pure
cherubic porcelain.

Tiny Tim beheld the man
and grabbed a plastic gun.
(His father often lectured him
upon The Castle Doctrine.)

In Santa's sack lay *Heavenly Piece*.
(He fumbled to confirm it.
Like any self-respecting Claus
he had a carry permit.)

So both invoked Amendment rights
they separately reckoned.
Toddler and Saint both stood their ground.
The First shot; then, the Second.

The plastic gun was not a toy
but crafted by Tim's mother,
who thoughtfully had fired up
her 3D copier.

So now two lie beside the tree
each in his Xmas red.
Saint Nicholas punches 9-1-1
before his phone goes dead.

Two sleeping parents hold their peace
behind their bedroom door.
A pit bull plays with a RoboMouse
stirring upon the floor.

The Very Last Supper

> *79% of recent college graduates do not support affirmative action . . . . Their dream dinner guest is Jesus Christ.*
> — Harris poll

They found Him
at Eternity Online, then downloaded
in His image from davinci.com.

He checked His Palm Pilate, said
sure, His stigmata were still open, but
could He bring a friend?

They only had service for twelve.

"He handles
his own silver."

That evening, in the vestibule, you could
pick them out right away, the only two robes
without data ports. For once, John
didn't say a word.

"Totally wireless," Tom whispered.
"Neural interface."

Turned out JC hadn't read
The Eleventh Commandment
or *Men Who Love Too Much.*
Judas shuffled away
from the buffet, when he found out

nobody named kids Judas anymore.

Matt got JC alone by the window, said
he was with the IHS, auditing
performance artists.
"You want *my* input? Lose
the hair, tattoo the thorns.
It's all deductible."

When they finally ran out of wine, Jimmy asked,
"Can you do a Merlot?"

Jesus shrugged. "This year OK?"

"You *can't* make a 27 C.E.?
Or you *won't*?"

He smoothed things over, lied
about the vintage, about the camels
and needles, let them know
He'd come to believe
in gated communities. Pete ashked
how He handled shecurity.

"Keyless. With retinal scans."

"Effing Alfa!"
"You the *man*!"

And Judas, surrounded
yet alone with his unspeakable
SATs, wondered why

his black ass'd been dragged
all the way down to hear
these future CEOs
blessing each other's brilliance —
until, leaning over that long table
of bodies and blood, he figured
this time he'd kiss them all.

Serving Free Lunches in the Basement of the Travelers Rest United Methodist Church

We smile between gray hair and double chins,
hand paper sacks and plates to all the kids.
Five volunteers together, underground,
to monitor our nation's charity.

We're charged to keep an inventory of
the carrot sticks, the flavored gelatins,
the applesauce containers, pudding pops,
and low-fat milk the boys refuse to drink.

Squat dusty windows kiss the ceiling, so
we look up, sideways, at our cemetery.
Carved granite stares from grass bleached by the sun.
On the linoleum, each orthopedic

shoe and tiny sneaker holds its bones
at what must be the level of the caskets.
But lost in sandwiches and Chocolate Moo
these Opies from *The Andy Griffith Show*

stay colorized in the fluorescent light.
From where they sit, the glass holds only sky.
They chew communal food beneath a sign
noting they should take nothing from the room.

They throw their vegetables away, before
returning to the gym for basketball.

Wiping their tables down with dripping rags,
we note the dates that follow every name.

The Heaven of Mistaken Assumptions

> *Behold, there appeared a chariot of fire, and horses of fire, and separated them, and Elijah went up by a whirlwind into heaven.*
> — 2 Kings 2:11

Here are all God's mistakes:
the Adolphs, the Evas,
Benito, Iago, the Duke
of Ferrara — the actual
and those imagined
by His better creations —
gathered together in this cacophony
of clouds and miserable manna
waiting for grace.

Which arrives, albeit
in modest measure. For even
these who have labored
under their dark, dire
assumptions have been assumed
to this special, if segregated, space.

What did You expect, My Son?

Who replies He was almost human
like them, once, yet not forsaken

while the Holy Ghost, nodding,
gazes with something akin to affection

at all those immaculate white robes —
even the ones with hoods.

Optics

for Ken McClane

Black is no color
and all of them.

White is all colors
and none of them.

So it's simply
a matter of reflection

and absorption, prism
and paper, prison

and sentence.

II

How

Hempstead, 1959

This August afternoon, we've driven back,
a full year after moving farther east,
to visit my first elementary school.

I'm a big boy now, through second grade.
My old friends won't be here for two more weeks.

And as my mother leads me through familiar
hallways, full of lost furniture, I lean
to touch the line of battered desks, fingers
entering carved graffiti near the inkwells,
look up at circular fluorescent lights. . . .

Now I'm back in the only classroom where
I'd ever feel unmitigated joy.

It's empty of everything except the blackboard.

But then tiny Miss Kestenbaum appears,
my first-grade teacher. What is this ancient eight-
year-old to do?

                                        My mother drops my hand
and I find myself running footloose toward her,
falling into her arms as if she were —
What? A second mother, only younger?

Yet even as I hug her through my tears,

burying my left ear between her breasts,
I see the windowsill's newest begonia,
not knowing whether to face the lights, or sun.

Vigor

1.
Fall 1960, and a new
school year! Just think of it —
nine-year-old boys, strutting around,
appropriating shit-

faced Boston accents, shouting *This*
country must move ahead
with viggah! To the sideways smiles
of teachers, Mom and Dad,

even the principal. Weekends
to the Italian store-
keeper, who sold us Cokes, watched us
stuff comics (on a dare)

under our shirts. Stayed mute.
We were considered cute.

2.
I truly don't remember who
came up with it — but it
was in the "cafetorium."
In a New York minute

we all intoned *Our country must*
move ahead with viggah!
After a pause, revealing our
cleverness — *No niggahs!*

We went back to our three-cent milks,
nursing them in silence.
A PTA mom standing with
two white custodians

said nothing. But she heard.
They heard. They must have heard.

The Janitors' Concert

for John Beckford

Before we got there, they'd already folded
the long gray tables, stacking them a half-
dozen deep against the proscenium arch
of the cafetorium. The metal
chairs we usually ate our lunches in

waited for us — empty rows straighter
than any ruler — as we single-filed
class by class, for the awards assembly
marking our graduation to junior high.

I know I won something, like everyone else.
But what I remember is sitting exactly where
Bob Preble had stomped a half-pint milk container
in May, raising a white geyser of laughter.

Now June filled the room with nearly summer.
And then — on that high stage where Mr. Lambert
once held himself cruciform on the curtains
when our band got the music even more wrong
than usual —

                                        the four of them appeared
still in their gray overalls. We wondered where
their barrels were — the ones with tiny wheels —
what last colossal mess they had to clean up.

Walking slowly, leaning into a small arc

widened by their smiles, they started to sing —
these unbarbered men now a barbershop
quartet, their bright voices turning their uniform
drab into the color of sound no symphony

has managed to dim for me in fifty years.
I still can see their faces — black Irish, like
my father, three o'clock shadow — sunlight
from the windows lining the west wall.
Dust motes grace notes suspended in the air

we breathed. They'd probably grown up in New
York City — 1920s, along with that
song *Heart of My Heart* — offering their first music
now to us, to hold in our left shirt pockets

along with our new transistor radios
mimicking their packs of cigarettes.
And when they finished, applause burst from us —
our childhood making its way through our hands
leaving us with nothing but what we'd risen

to become, and no way to know it.

A Short History of Stone Age Rock

for Jack Brimm

Young Elvis (waist up) on *Ed Sullivan*,
Danny and the Juniors at the hop,
Chuck Berry talking smack to Beethoven,
Jerry Lee's keyboard karate chops,

Gene Chandler's standup guy, The Duke of Earl,
The Coasters giving fathers yakkity yaks,
The Marvelettes' melodious pleas for mail,
Da Doo Ron Ron (a synonym for sex)

while Ricky's driving tweener girls insane.
Poor Buddy Holly (and Big Bopper), lost
to future elegies by Don McLean.
The Beach Boys, fitting Bach with dual exhausts

and parking him near Spector's wall of sound
until The Beatles came, and knocked it down.

A Visitation

Yes, there's something the dead are keeping back.
— "The Witch of Coös"

October 18, 1990: Beech Mountain, NC

At thirty-nine, resigned to childlessness,
we took a holiday that early fall.
A hundred forty miles, four thousand feet
above our home, we stopped in early winter.
Flurries had just begun to stain the streets.
Stunted maples, oaks already stripped,
leaves frozen in the driveway's pothole puddles.
Our so-called cabin, sharpening the wind
seemed specially designed for downdrafts — ashes
filling the room at gusty intervals
while nothing in the fireplace would burn
and I thought what the hell, and closed the damper.

What the hell! We made love in the whirlpool,
the only place above sixty degrees.

That night, the storm kept screaming in my sleep
while you dreamed of my father — dead since June,
sitting a scant six inches from your feet,
his silence filling you with joy and grief.

The next month, when we found out you were pregnant,
and ten days after that, the baby lost,
you swore you knew what brought him to that height
and what you knew now, he'd already known.

Family Dining

Should I have seen this coming? Used Pampers
littering a parking lot's dead heat
are never a good sign. I could've had
a quiche across the street.

You want a hamburger, you pay the price.
But in the twilight zone, well after lunch,
I found an empty alcove near the john.
My food's up, when a bunch

of kids — children and parents — blunder in,
passing six empty booths to sit behind me.
I feel their rumps thump through the common back.
One. Two. Three.

The boy stands on the vinyl, eyes my fries.
"He's hungry," Mom explains. I literally
can't complain when he caterwauls, because
THIS IS FAMILY

DINING. At least his diaper isn't at
nose level. Ah, the agonies and joys
I've never known! The waitress, six months gone,
coos, "He's soo cute!" The boy's

finished before he's started, up again.
This kid is poetry in motion — I'm
the page his greasy hands are writing on.
My shirt's long past its prime

anyway, I guess. When I stand to leave,
Dad's fumbling with a newborn's underside.
What will the waitress wipe their table with?
Their booth's a suicide

bombing — condiments stuck on body parts
to make a colorful catastrophe.
Mom shrugs her shoulders, says *My life*. I nod,
more or less vertically.

My food was edible. I'm still alive.
So when the cashier/waitress asks me, twice,
"Enjoy your meal?" I leave a decent tip
and no advice.

How

many years has it taken me
to realize you, Barbara,
are my best story?

I've given my life
to that lofty country where the truth
is no excuse, even
at that left, sinister margin
when every fact, face will leave us
nothing at all.

But from that almost-first
meeting, at a summer dive, at midnight,
when I honestly believed your sorority sister
with the bobbed hair and pantsuit
was your implausibly short, silent
boyfriend (till I happily
discerned, through a dozen daiquiris'
daze, his purse)

to when I picked you up
at your parents' house and remembered
seeing you at the Beach Boys concert
four months and three hundred miles
earlier, and told you where
you'd sat, and the color
and cut of your winter coat
though on that March evening

I'd never seen your face

to finally today, nearly thirty
years later, when your mother marches headstone-sober
into our bedroom at dawn and asks who
in the world you are
and speaking yourself through your sleep
you ask back *Who do you think I am*
and she happily decides
A good friend —

how
in hell or heaven
can I better that?

Long Island, 2001

Ornament

for Linda Julian, 1946-2003

I think you'd like it. You collected pigs,
the sillier the better — charm bracelets,
aprons, bedroom slippers, T-shirts, fig-
urines, spoonrests, refrigerator magnets.
This sow — two roses (red) behind her ears
spread like the wimple of The Flying Nun —
with a dazed piglet inside her basket-purse,
looking up like a first-semester freshman.

Her pompom tail points at an angel's face
hovering in mid-tree, lost in a book.
First food, then reading, lost in your last days.
The cat you gave us comes to take a look
at this most recent Christmas ornament
hanging upon a green bough, slightly bent.

The Mass of August

We're sitting on our deck, in that last light
of a summer's setting, feeling that delicious
heaviness of the horizon in our limbs.
Not unable to move our butts, but — well,
these Martha Stewart chairs *are* comfortable.
We'll shoot the breeze, and let it do the work
of motion, through the beds we've mulched and Preened.
Just maintenance now, thank goodness, which we do
in sudden bursts of energy — that strike
like thunderstorms, you say, leaving us soaked
with happiness we never understood
at thirty-five.
Is joy itself a weight
meted out in birthdays and inertia?
I used to move for the sheer hell of it,
running ten miles at noon, felling stray oaks
with a handsaw. Sometimes I still do.
But now, those moods are mercifully infrequent.

Each summer, as we sit outside our home,
my legs grow heavier. But happier, too.
Sloth, my favorite sinful animal,
still manages to get by on three toes.
Economy, as Emerson might say,
or was it Thoreau? I won't look it up,
since all my books are within walking distance.

Leaves tug the sky, as if that single cloud
were the white beard of God — a Renaissance
marquis who manages not to be miffed
at what attendants deem a deadly insult.
He's learning not to puff His chest so much.

Today, my own hands look as old as God's —
crowned not with thorns, but with the blooms of age.
My doctor called them *fleurs de cimetière*.
"You're not a stone," he smiled. "We'll all get them."

I guess in graveyards the best stones become us —
diamonds in our settings, on display,
hidden in boxes never to be opened
beneath (and not upon) this dark green felt.

Some days, the planet turns to poetry
while it darkens — or at least light verse.
Off to our left, green beans are blackening.
Tomatoes still hold oranges and reds.
A garden tells us what God would have done
if only He'd not trusted us so much. . . .

I could do something, but why start a trend?
The vegetables will have to wait till morning.
The grass, though going nowhere, will be cut.

Dover Beach (Barbados)

a sort of mournful cosmic last resort
— Anthony Hecht, "The Dover Bitch"

We didn't stay there — we went more upscale
for our vacation week. But we drove by.
Between Miami Beach and Rendezvous,
it's been the Class B Hotel of the Year.
Three stars — "a perfect fit for families
and honeymooners alike." Too bad for us.
We've been alone together forty years.

The Calais Block boasts air conditioning,
uninterrupted views of Caribbean
turquoise, softly breaking on white beaches.
Covered balconies, TV with cable,
double beds, and full-sized kitchenettes —
for only US 200 a night!
The Rasta lifeguard's complimentary.
Free beach towels, just as long as you don't lose them.
You pay for ice cream, snorkels, boogie boards.
A sidewalk leads to bars and slot machines
for any soul who needs a note of sadness.

At our full service Platinum Coast resort
the melancholy, long, withdrawing roar's
more like a whisper. Menacing manchineels
are ringed with red around their trunks, so guests
won't stand beneath them in the rain and get
a dripping case of contact dermatitis.
(Think poison ivy that's been weaponized.)

Enough Brits come here so the waiters don't
look puzzled if you ask for tea in pots.
No insects — but the sparrows and goldfinches
flutter on every unattended plate
at the outdoor breakfasts. Who can blame them?
Eggs Benedict to die for, flying fish,
French toast and tarts — and not a cat in sight.

We make our days up as we go along.
We'll visit a plantation still intact
from 1658, behold some ruins,
and then repair to the spa pool. We'll drink
rum punch, proclaim that Life Is Good, and stare
into our sunset. Barbados doesn't have
much of an army, ignorant or not.

For the time being, Sophocles is deaf.
Nobody's bitching. Everyone's polite
to every color. Each parish is a saint
and every Sunday every church is full.

Fruit

So many years ago, in Greece,
Athens, I think, or Mykonos
maybe, we stood out in the street
market, early morning, looking

for our breakfast — and we beheld
tomatoes, grapes, held on a wicker
salver by the most sun-wizened
woman we'd ever seen, not much

older than we are now, and we
pointed to what we wanted, reached —
but she pulled away, limping a
little *No No* — probably

her only English — scolding us
toward what looked too blemished, on
the verge of rotten, rancid, but
possibly the richest of

them all — and we shook our heads,
convinced she was intent on cheating
a pair of dumb Americans
who didn't know a fig about the world.

For Our 70th Birthdays

Mine's January, yours is June.
Both months will be upon us soon
for it's December — and the snow
at breakfast seems so apropos.

Then, of our threescore years and ten
L-X-X won't come again.
Just do the math — and you'll discern
that leaves no leaves that haven't turned.

But since, for now, we're both still here,
things aren't bleak as might appear.
Let's have our dinner at *Cote D'Or* —
as long as they still serve at four.

III

Green Hair

Green Hair

But any girl who talked as coherently as [Jane Austen's Elizabeth Bennet] would be stared at as though she had green hair.
— Northrop Frye, *The Educated Imagination* (1964)

Now everybody's here — the cops,
the local TV camera crews,
the surplus paramedic teams —
surrounding this

implausibility in black,
this fourteen-, maybe fifteen-year-
old Goth, festooned with safety pins.
She has green hair

nearly down to her navel ring.
And she's explaining, in a voice
fit for a new high-budget *Pride
and Prejudice*,

how the old Buick ran them off
the switchback two-lane, coming straight
at them, the wrong side of the curve.
It was too late

for Brian to do anything
but aim his pickup past the shoulder
at dogwoods and the underbrush.
They flipped over,

rolled down the hillside to the creek,

or almost, that big willow tree
crumpling his door. Broke both his legs.
She pulled him free,

took out her cell, punched 9-1-1.
Then dragged herself a quarter mile
straight downstream, to the other car —
a smoking pile

of moans. "The poor old gentleman
experienced a heart attack."
Her pierced lips shape the words. She crawled
into the Buick,

told him they'd leave together. Soon.
She held his hand. Ten minutes later
the cops hauled down a portable
defibrillator.

So everybody's here (except
the rescued), staring at this kid —
not for her hair, not for her words —
for what she did.

Cross Dressers

God only knew why they'd sought out his church
for the detritus of their Saturdays.

As pastor, he was always first one there
on Sunday mornings. Lately he'd been parking
in the bleak darkness just before the dawn
to police the symbol of the risen Christ —

remove the Clemson cap, or produce bag
with TROJAN Sharpied on it, vertically,
before the congregation would arrive.

On other nights, they'd focus farther down —
suspending a brassiere hooked from behind
or wrapping where the Savior's waist would be
with Luvs or Cottonelle.

                                        But when they'd perched
a Budweiser on the end of either arm
he rummaged in the pockets of his coat
and fit his gloves over the twin glass necks
thumbs up — and left them for his unsuspecting
flock (and his tormentors), hoping that
like Son and Father, they could stand a joke.

Gas Ghazaller

circa 2007

He barrel-asses through the slush. His right.
His bumper broadly trumpets RUSH IS RIGHT.

So what if SUVs don't come in green?
George Bush can find Alaskan gushers. Right?

Who wants a *car*? Size matters, doesn't it?
The hell with laws. Ordnance crushes, right?

His counter-clockwise proof is in the plumbing.
American Standard always flushes right.

I think he's stopped — enjoying Nature's call.
Unzipped to baptize (By George!) bushes right.

SPEED LIMIT ENFORCED BY AIRCRAFT

Fighter aces become cubicle-bound drone operators.
— Edward Helmore (*Guardian*, August 23, 2009)

Drones flown.
Afghanistan
unmanned.
Crones moan.

No more?
No war?
Soar o'er
Route 4!

Screen clear.
Seen here
on cue
Subaru —

blue ass
too fast.
Enforce
perforce

now.
How?

POW!

Wow.

Manic Regressive

February 28, 2017

Yes, our planet's always been
bipolar, its head
beclouded, incessantly spinning, but this
is beyond bleak or balmy —
blizzards devoured by days
in the eighties, with tornados
and droughts for dessert.

Still, the waters are rising,
glaciers waving goodbye,
islands disappearing like necklaces
during Mardi Gras, and we're all
beating our bare breasts, falling down
drunk on ignorance or knowledge,
waiting for Ash Wednesday.

Touring the Holocaust Museum with Martha Stewart

"Lampshades you can make
at home. But this
cairn of shoes, which you might
relegate to your closet, could be
a fitting memorial to every guest
you've ever insulted. Before we leave
the sleeping quarters, please note
the *faux bain* —
an impressive addition
to any master suite.

"This boxcar, of course, overpowers
most living rooms, but makes
a marvelous garden shed — if left
unpainted, complementing the redolence
of your *merde locale.*
And the man — excuse me — *person*hole
cover from Warsaw, enhanced
by a welded bayonet, can
become the classical sundial
you'd never buy for yourself. . . ."

He was hoping she'd stay
till the end, or return
with a camera crew, but she or her dead
ringer didn't — preferring, evidently, her domestic arts

to his own thoughts or to Hitler's.

Still, he peers over the privacy fence
around Dr. Mengele's dock — remembering
a cast of thousands
cut up like starfish nobody ever figured
grew back.

Black Friday at Inner Spring

The barracudas selling beds
before they've even breakfasted
the day after Thanksgiving, said
"Sleep six years! Interest free!"

Young mothers, lining up at dawn
for special deals, free of their spawn,
incanted, with a joyful yawn,
Sleep six years, interest free.

The trophy wife from Malibu
(accompanied, alas, by Lou)
sneered, "What've you got to help *him* to
sleep six years, interest free?"

The battered woman who would kill
to keep her boyfriend sober, still
swiped his Discover card, so they'll
sleep six years, interest free.

And men who've suffered heart attacks
pursuing beasts that have two backs
have sadly come to face the facts:
Sleep, one way or the other, interest free.

Manikins for Dummies

A Poem for the Rest of Us!®

An empty dress demands an empty suit.
It's lonely in this prison of plate glass
awaiting interest, like a prostitute
in Amsterdam. Indifferent shoppers pass.

A dummy without a manikin is like
an Eve without an Adam, Lois Lane
without Clark Kent, a fish without a bike.
A single figure, staring through the pane

at the ever-moving world, entire.
Now put yourself in her shoes, or in his.
Even the impercipient require
if not Pygmalion's metamorphosis

company of a sort — a mime to share
the silence, a fellow rack's reflected stare.

OUTLOOK FOR TEMPORAL CREATURES BLEAK

In Heaven, daily newspapers
are exercises in
nostalgia. Copy editors —
gruff, cherubic — spread green

wings, glowing like a parakeet's,
keeping them suspended
over all miscaptioned athletes.
Every blesséd morning

enormous gatherings of shrouds,
sheet lightning, thunderous
obituaries, beetle-browed
carriers hit the street.

Hear their *extra, extra*'s
beat on these umbrellas.

Finished

"What are you drawing, Pumpkin?"
"I don't know — I'll decide
when I'm finished!" And the so-called
grownups giggle, because it's so
Godawful cute, which is to say, appropriately
incompetent, but isn't that what
we're doing each moment? Making
it up as we go along. Truth be told,

Pumpkin (not her real name) is drawing inside
a drawing, inside *The Greenville News*, inside
BOMB KILLS FOURTEEN CHILDREN.
Predictably enough, we children of God love
surprises, smashing a pumpkin. Gone, it
flattens to a halfway decent sonnet.

IV

Fearful Symmetry

The Great American Sonnet

To break the pentameter — that was the first heave.
— Ezra Pound, *Canto LXXXI*

These days, it must be multicultural —
replete with chickens, wheelbarrows and rain
of course, but vegetarian. No bull.
A rainbow coalition of the sane

forsaking English for its own street cred —
just "plain American, which cats and dogs
can read," as the Divine Miss M once said
to Presbyterians and demagogues.

Add Ku Klux Klansmen, ironing their sheets.
Throw in some gender-benders, sporting ties
strategically displayed to emphasize
their cleavage. Ballerinas wearing cleats.

A compost heap. Scannable, but terse.
Some Fascist peristalsis. In reverse.

Invitation

Good morning, Neighbors!

Those of you
who have been looking forward to
our Ladies Shooting Spree tonight
please text or email so I might
reserve a dedicated lane
at City Arsenal (off Main).

If need be, you can rent a gun —
I'd recommend a Remington.

The targets are $1.00 per —
imagine they're adulterers!
Or bring your own, if you'd prefer.

Come as you are. No special dress.
So glad you guys can make it!

— Tess

Elegy

In all societies, death constitutes a cultural event . . . .
— Mark Strand and Eavan Boland,
The Making of a Poem

The muses sentenced him to a cultural event
because *Poetry* still believes in the cultural event penalty

because a cultural event is the mother of beauty
and thus a Family Value, like the Second Amendment
or the right to bare and lose feet.

Dangling from a noose in Nevada,
he hung on like a cultural event
even though such waltzing was not easy, while
his porkpied choreographer sang, "I am become
a cultural event, the destroyer of worlds!"

I think he'd spent too much time
with those giant mushrooms.

Eventually a cultural event on a very pale horse
cantered into the valley of the shadow
of an even bigger Cultural Event
where rode the six hundred (theirs not to reason why).

I had not thought a cultural event had undone so many.

But because I, like any good American, could not stop
for a cultural event, he kindly stopped his swaying, horseless carriage
for me — when I looked up, and I beheld

a cultural event in the sky.

We weren't in Nevada any more
or even a Norton.

"So how do you like your blueeyed boy
Mister Cultural Event?" I Googled.

And the webmaster answered,
"This is TheBlackWidow.com, a cultural event."

Second Thoughts

I'm just about to ink the bottom line
on a compact luxury sedan. The sales
rep, fresh from college, vaguely serpentine,
raises his polished head, and then exhales.

"A guy *your* age? You should be living large!"
He jerks his big thumb towards the showroom aisle,
towards something luminescent as the barge
that floated Cleopatra down the Nile.

"Good God," I say. He fingers the gold cross
that's fallen out the front of his golf shirt.
"Would Jesus drive a little POS?
Not if He really wants you to convert!"

The Holy Spirit moves me, says, "I'll pass.
Jerusalem's accessible by ass."

Fearful Symmetry

It's time to bring all cats indoors and keep them there.
—John Balzar, "Too Many Cats," *Los Angeles Times*

I won't even keen for my furniture.
The reupholsterers can cover for me.
But there'd be the rodential problem, moles, voles
turning American lawns into acres of individual
slices of green Swiss. Though
the snakes would take care
of it, eventually, restoring our Edens
to their original good
and mediocre.
Regrettably, then, there'd be
the serpentine problem, copperheads
knotted under the throats of our outdoor
spigots, like designer neckties — until
the teleherpetologists took
over, culling the most venomous
who'd knowingly refuse to bite the tongues of the glossolaliacants
and die. Then, of course, we'd have
that problem, but Christ
would take care of it, leaving
his little lambkin at home, safely outside.

Burgerdämmerung

In the beginning was money,
and gentrification was good.
So the Spirit of Urban Renewal
said, "Eve's Diner stays! Understood?"

But soon there was trouble in Eden.
Some snake told a customer fibs.
His faith in her twin patties shaken,
the first man embraced a McRib.

The neighborhood followed McAdam
swiftly, though often unseen.
Now nothing's afloat but McNoah's,
drowning the local cuisine.

And then, in His infinite wisdom
and rainbow-inspiring view,
the corporate head, a McYahweh,
declared all He'd done was for you.

Customer Assistance

an automated villanelle

We value every caller. Please stand by.
Listen closely for menu directives. . . .
I'm sorry. I don't understand. Let's try

to get a few things straight. Can you provide
the full nine-digit zip code where you live?
Thanks so much, Mr. Allen. Please stand by. . . .

Do you know you're our first priority?
Say *yes* or press 1 for affirmative. . . .
I'm sorry. I don't understand. Let's try

this one more time. . . . Okay. Now verify
your primary account by pressing 5. . . .
We value every caller. Please stand by.

Remember: It is a crime to falsify
or fabricate the data that you give. . . .
I'm sorry. I don't understand. Let's try

to maximize your user quality. . . .
Please hold for our next representative.
We value every caller. Please stand by.
Please hold —

Tech Support

Yellowstone National Park

We've stopped for geysers and the good Flush Ts.
You can't get any wireless out here
but Barbara thumbs her TracPhone, hopefully.
A solitary bison soon appears,

eating his way toward the parking lot.
Parched grass leads him to INFORMATION STATION
and its punctuating arrow — not
an inch between his rump and the pointing sign.

His shaggy head is shaking No No No.
He's strictly analog, and not IT.

Inevitable brown, descending, slow.

At least he doesn't say, "Reboot and see
if that corrects your problem. Good luck. *Ciao.*"

I think we've been reduced to postcards now.

Organ Recitals

for Keller Freeman

Sam's bunion doesn't even let him walk
for long enough to get his dog to pee.

"My prostate seems to think *I* shouldn't pee,"
Tim scowled, straight at his trousers.

"*You* should talk."
Dee pulled a diaper from her purse. "Don't gawk.
I wear these bad boys everywhere."

"Now, Dee,
You call *that* trouble? What about my knee?
I'm on my third, and all it does is ache."
Priscilla sniffled, lifting up her skirt
to show her latest scar.

"Top this," Frank said,
arthritic fingers fumbling with his shirt.
"Quadruple bypass, after a Code Red!"

"Code Blue," their waitress smiled. "Frank's such a flirt."

Tim grimaced. "He should quit while he's ahead."

UNLIMITED OPPORTUNITIES STATEWIDE

South Carolina Department of Corrections,
full-page newspaper ad

The pale elbow serenely rests upon
a holstered non-slip handled black baton

as if a symphony's about to start.
FACILITIES ARE NOW STATE OF THE ART.

Beyond the foreground, all's an orange blur
that could be violinists, prisoners,

or both. Below, the list of benefits:
3 weeks vacation, 13 requisite

holidays, and medical insurance.
SALARY BASED ON YOUR EXPERIENCE.

In law enforcement, or in solitary?
Incarceration's our key industry.

Just try a few bars. They'll tell you the score
so everyone can face the music now.

V

Joyville

Joyville

with apologies to Ernest Thayer

There is no mud in Joyville, because
our land never truly cries, not for long, and yet
there's no lack of good water.
Amber waves, purple majesties stretch
from one shining sea to
another, both in manifest
sight — every tempered glass house
ruthlessly clear. Gray seems merely
the unauthorized merger of black
and white, a momentary lapse
in good corporate management.

So the sun rises and sets, each day,
upon deep green, dazzling as diamonds.
Here's home plate.
Palmettos and hemlocks shake hands.
In this division, there's no such thing
as weather. The boxwoods fulfill
their uniform destiny, a manicured charity
bracing each foundation. Buttercups fade
only to butterflies, orisons rising
to performance bonuses.

But we're still watching the game
on the world's biggest screen
in the world's biggest stadium.
We'll root for the home team, Joyville,
our unrestricted free agents

landing in Kabul, in Kandahar, in Damascus,
and it's a shame
nobody's winning.

Kill the Empire! Kill the Empire!

Rubble hunkers like snow
in the stricken streets
and nothing melts, no matter
how much we holler from the skybox
because this is January, even in Joyville,
the land of big-league hardball
the land of three strikes and you're out.

Belief

No belief in the Viagra?
— subject line, unsolicited email message

No — I want to give Reply
With History — Aver
I do — in the Viagra born
Of Judaism — there

Upon His final power Pole
Beneficent — to bear
Good News — transcending Time and Space
Indubitably Firm —

Adequate — *Erect* — just as
ED proclaimed her Host —
Peering — praying — from within
Her Amherst lookout — Post —

And as the gaunt Survivalist
In North Dakota said —
A Rosary of hollow-points
Around his Neck — like Lead —

I'm entitled — *to my Beliefs!*
And I believe — in guns
And Auschwitz — Abu Ghraib — Darfur —
Guantanamo — the Son

Of Sam — Mistakes and Deity —

Yes

Trumpery, trumpery!
Senator John McCain
Hearing *heroic* means
Not getting caught

Caught himself wondering
Unpresidentially
Can this twit be even
Worse than I thought?

Roadside Calvary, Flagpole Presiding

due west of Washington, DC

Supersized, it seemed a little strange
at first, Old Glory. Then I realized
trussed up here hung America. Our two
states of the spirit, left and right — thieves crossed,
clutching the splinters of our government.

One penitent, the other not so much —
wraiths framing a high ideal inclined to die
above our heads. It stimulates our faith,
clear as an HOV lane to a shining
city on a hill — concrete, and never there.

Shooting the Snowman

December 2018

No, I'm not talking about
a duffer's impossible dream
or Tiger's worst nightmare.
I'm talking about the neighbor
through the naked woods —
sweetgums, oaks, poplars —
who, after yesterday's blizzard, emboldened
by the electrical outage
on this dazzling morning, took out
his muzzleloader and fired
straight for the coals, then
for the button, and finally
the corncob pipe.

Who's to say what
triggered his mind? Maybe he beheld the man —

no, a strange *creature* who'd crossed
the border, descending in darkness upon
his way of life, which
like mine at that moment
lacked all the customary power
he wanted back.

Once More,
The Sound of Music

Live-on-tape TV for the holidays!
The sets are lavish, large, and multiple.
It's like peering into Biltmore House
before they started charging folks admission.

And Carrie Underwood's more Julie Andrews
than — well, Julie Andrews. The seven kids?
Not only can they sing, but if cuteness
is a cancer, every one is terminal.

Von Trapp — dark, gruff, and incorruptible —
strum-bumbles his guitar around the shoals
of lechery, to seem semi-convincing
as Captain, father, lover, patriot.

At the convent, Mother Superior's
a penguin of color with the voice of God,
belting out a multicultural
overture to love, for Her blond novice.

And, after that family sing-along
celebrating Anschluss, as the Lucky
Nine deceive storm troopers, spirit themselves
to church, to footpaths, then to Switzerland,

the hills are alive with the sound of Auschwitz.

Adieu, Adieu, Adieu —
To Jew, and Jew, and Jew.
Nobody knows — plenty of plausible
deniability to go around.
Should we expect the Captain to bring down

the Reich? Heil Hitler with his middle finger?
Sometimes the only sensible thing to do
is get the hell out of Dodge, or Austria.
In a new century, another country,

upstairs my wife is ironing snowflakes
for our *Nutcracker* party. And I hum
Me, the guy I plan to save
Canada's not far to run.
1971, 2019.
Some songs you just can't get out of your head.

Lessons from the Dead

December 2020

They Zoom from their refrigerated trucks:
You are the slowest students on God's earth.
We're sick of lecturing, you stupid fucks.
They Zoom from their refrigerated trucks
that, for the record, Purgatory sucks.
And now their message buffers. For what it's worth
they won't stop Zooming from their hopeless trucks.
But we're the slowest students on God's earth.

Mending News

with apologies to Robert Frost

Something there is that doesn't love a war —
European or wherever — on the tube
that, for a decade, hasn't had a tube.
We need less breaking and more mending news.

Picture old Movietones run in reverse
where buildings reassemble magically,
crushed bodies levitating from debris,
the bullet a blunt needle stitching flesh,

a mushroom cloud intact Hiroshima
at dawn. And no, I'm not an advocate
for Happy News — feel-good finales that
follow the last commercial with a Fido

wagging his tail from Kharkiv to Lviv
after his westbound owners couldn't find him
or the insouciant Persian seraphim
purring beneath Mariupol's rubble.

No, what I want is just a world made whole
after each so-called surgical attack.
That would be good both going and coming back
for all us sorry old stone savages.

For the Lost Fathers

Today I'm vacuuming the bedroom carpet —
long overdue — with all the loose furniture
lifted aside, the floor empty as my mind
could make it. I look toward the bureau bookcase
at the Polaroid of my father, pretending
to play an upright piano — a silly gag
a few years before he died — while the word
forgotten seems to breathe from the machine
as if it were a solitary lung
laboring after sixty years of smoking.

I turn it off. I'm one of the few alive
who know his hands couldn't find the middle *C*.

So I can't help imagining this image
beheld by others, centuries from now —
the future holding music visible
but never there. A silent lie. And then

the picture itself, dissolving into dust,
or mold, or fire, within a world that has
forgotten Polaroids, and me, and must
and will forget every last one of us.

I turn the vacuum on, get back to work

and find, next to my father, the blue spine
of Jim McConkey's *Court of Memory*,

concluded by "What Kind of Father Am I?"

And in an unrehearsed *recitativo*
both men insist: *Fathers will be forgotten.*
But the present always will recall,
remember someone now not of this world —
who once recalled, in his or her own turn,
another being from a world more distant.
Invisible minds holding invisible hands
across the great courtyard of time itself
that does and will reach to infinity
in both directions, making the universe
once and for all whole as the mind of God.

Marcescence in March

Whenever my wife and I abandon speech
to drive the Blue Ridge Parkway, intent upon
a picturesque late lunch, replete with wine
and lingering snow, she'll single out a beech
along the roadside — *Fergus grandiflora*
still clinging to its faded parchment pages.
Its words? Gone with the wind, Mt. Mitchell wheezes.
An open book, still blank as Ibsen's Nora.

Botanists insist marcescent leaves
protect the buds from winter deer and cold.
For us, they give the sun a place to gild
before spring hooks the eye only to heaves
of green. Persistence, celebrate the here
and now! Then, like your kindred spirits, disappear.

Clearcut

Travelers Rest, South Carolina, 2022

Nothing's left standing to see.
Morning rain makes a melody
of mud in this sawdusted city
of stumps — every tree harvested
for next season's firewood,
newspapers, novels,
buttresses, barrels.

Still, it seems almost greening
walking here in the waning
weeks of winter, gleaning
what will become of what was
from only the nothing that is —
in the new afterlife
someone will find enough.

Here

where the past
gilds the grass

and the bones
blossom stones

and brass plaques
piggyback

upon urns
that confirm

where the comely
and the homely —

all the births
of this earth —

come home.

About the Author

Gilbert Allen is the author of eight collections of poems and two collections of short stories. His work has received the Robert Penn Warren Prize from *The Southern Review*, The Amon Liner Award from *The Greensboro Review*, the Rainmaker Award from *Zone 3*, the Nancy Dew Taylor Award from the *Emrys Journal*, and Special Mention for a Pushcart Prize. His poems have been featured on *The Writer's Almanac*, *Poetry Daily*, *Verse Daily*, and *Your Daily Poem*. In 2014 he was elected to the South Carolina Academy of Authors, the state's literary hall of fame. He lives on Paris Mountain with his wife, the educator and environmental activist Barbara Allen. He is the Bennette E. Geer Professor of Literature Emeritus at Furman University.

www.ingramcontent.com/pod-product-compliance
Lightning Source LLC
Chambersburg PA
CBHW030428310726
48979CB00009B/1661/J

* 9 7 8 1 9 3 9 5 7 4 4 2 8 *